DORIS
TROUBLE

WRITTEN BY MAX DANN
ILLUSTRATED BY BETTINA GUTHRIDGE

Campbell's really big problems began some time after Doris moved into the house three doors down from his. I mean, he'd always had little problems of one sort or another.

Things like how to make a glass of chocolate milk in the middle of the night without anybody hearing him. Or the problem of how he could sit in the bathtub for twenty minutes every day and still keep his hair dry. Or how to get his shoes on and off again without undoing the laces. You know—that sort of thing.

But Doris was much more of a problem than any of those problems. Doris was trouble. Doris liked the exciting life. Which was all right in itself he supposed, only she insisted that Campbell join in.

Doris was always wanting him to do dangerous things—swinging from trees in his swimsuit, performing trapeze acts on the clothesline, crawling around underneath the house looking for spiders, patting wild dogs (corgis, poodles, etcetera), walking behind the counter in the corner store without asking first. There was no end of daring feats she made Campbell perform.

It was no good not wanting to. Doris didn't take no for an answer.

And there was no way of avoiding Doris.

Campbell wondered why it had to be him. Why did he have to be her friend? Why not Robert? Robert was much more of a daredevil than Campbell. Robert was more Doris's type.

Campbell's favorite place in all the world was his very own room. Sometimes, he'd just sit in there for hours at a time, not doing anything but looking at the wallpaper. Life was peaceful and calm, and perfectly safe in his room.

He liked to spend a lot of time there. He had a lot of things he could do in there. Sorting out his stamp collection, sharpening his colored pencils, reading the atlas. You know—that sort of thing. Quiet, peaceful, safe things.

Doris thought it was unhealthy, sitting in there all day long. No excitement, no fresh air, no hustle or bustle, no noise, no nothing.

Last Saturday afternoon things began to look even worse than usual.

Doris arrived with her cricket set. She slid his window open and climbed in.

"Here I am!" she said.

Campbell didn't look up. He was sitting on the floor in the middle of a very important operation. It was almost a matter of life and death as far as he was concerned.

He was trying to paste a picture of the Great Barrier Reef into his Social Studies scrapbook. He always got nervous using rubber cement. The smallest thing could go wrong and you'd end up with a disaster on your hands.

"When will you be ready?" Doris asked.

Campbell was trying his hardest not to listen. He almost had it in place. Lining it up, sliding it into position...

"Can't you hurry up?"

That did it. His hand moved, the Great Barrier Reef slid across the page and landed on top of the Grampian Mountains. There was rubber cement all over the place. He'd smudged his writing, dropped the brush on the carpet—everything was ruined.

"Is that it? Have you finished now? Are you ready?"

"Ready? Ready to do what?"

"Ready to go and play cricket."

"I'm not going," he said. "I hate cricket."

"You don't really. You just pretend you do. I tell you what, I'll let you bat for a while this time."

Campbell sat on his bed and folded his arms. "I hate batting more than anything," he said.

"You have to come. I can't play by myself."

"No, I'm not going. Not in a thousand years." Campbell folded his arms even tighter.

"All right," Doris said.

She was climbing out the window, walking down the side of the house, heading for the shed. He could hear her out there, moving this and that around. What was she doing out there? She was looking for something. The rope? That was it! She was going to tie him up!

Campbell hated the rope. Even cricket was better than the rope. He ran across to the window and stuck his head out.

"I'll play!" he called out.

Campbell had to put his brown tweed coat on first. He put his coat on before he went anywhere. Unless it was very hot, of course, then he'd just carry it.

They went across to Mahoney's vacant lot. It was Doris's favorite place to play cricket. It was wedged in between an iron works on one side and a car wrecking yard on the other. Then at either end there were a couple of passing streets. They were almost as quiet as Mahoney's lot.

"I'm ready when you are," Doris shouted.

She had to shout. Campbell was standing so far away it was the only way he could have heard her. He liked to bowl from a long way off. It gave him time to get out of the way if it looked like she was going to hit the ball in his direction.

It was a slow game, especially for Doris. She only got to hit one every twenty minutes or so. It wasn't because she was such a bad hitter. It was Campbell. He didn't know how to bowl. He was probably the worst bowler in all of Spotswood. The ball went everywhere except where she happened to be standing. If she moved to the left, it'd end up on the right. If she went and stood on the right, over by the iron works wall, it'd bounce off down the left somewhere. He hadn't learned a thing in the whole three months she'd been training him.

"OK, it's your bat now."

"I don't want to bat," Campbell said, "you throw the ball too hard."

"This time I'll throw it soft."

There was only one thing worse than bowling, and that was batting. Doris always stood too close—and, besides, the bat wasn't big enough. The way Doris sent them down, it was like trying to hit bullets with an ice-cream stick. One day Campbell was going to invent a cricket bat the size of a kitchen table. Something big enough to stand behind.

She threw the first one down. *Whooooosh!* Campbell just had time to get out of the way.

Then the second one. *Ping!* That was even closer. Campbell really hated batting.

Another one! He had to dive on to his stomach that time.

"This one will be a slow one. I promise."
He didn't believe her.
"I double promise."
Campbell got ready. He had an idea. If he managed to hit it over Doris's head and get it on to the road behind her, it might just roll across the street and down into the drain. His problems would be over.
Slow! It was faster than the others. But it was too late to get out of the way. He was all set up to hit it. There was no time to do anything but take cover. *Wok!* He hit it! Well, actually, it really just happened to run into his bat while he was waving it around. It went so high it disappeared for a moment. Campbell crouched down and covered his head with his hands. He knew it was going to come back down and land on his head.

But it didn't. It landed somewhere else altogether. Somewhere worse. Somewhere much worse.

Inside the wrecking yard.

He could tell by the thud it made hitting one of the old tires. Doris ran up and shook his hand.

"That was a great shot."

"I'm sorry about losing your ball, Doris." He didn't sound all that sorry.

"That's all right. You didn't lose it. We know where it is."

"We could come back on Monday when Mr. Caruso opens up again, and ask him for a look around," Campbell suggested.

"We don't have to wait that long. We'll climb over and get it now."

Campbell looked up at the fence. It was that criss-cross cyclone wire, with two different types of barbed wire running across the top. Campbell could have stood on his shoulders three times, and he still couldn't have made it all the way up there. He could feel one of his dizzy spells coming on.

"It's too high," he said.

"These fences are a cinch to climb over."

"What about the dog? There's a big dog in there."

"Mr. Caruso only drops him off at night. Besides, you have to climb over—you hit it in. That's the rules."

11

They started to climb. If he was careful he could squash the toe of his sneakers into the little squares without getting them stuck.

It was a long way to the top. Then when he got there he had to squeeze through the lines of barbed wire. He must have gotten his coat snagged fifty times before he finally got past them. Doris was already walking around looking at all the junk by the time he made it down on the other side.

What a mess! Campbell had never noticed it before. But then he'd never been standing in the middle of it before. He'd never seen so many stupid bits and pieces all in one place.

Long round things, small lumpy bits, rusty doors, old wheels, bent-up exhaust pipes, torn seats, loose steering wheels, odd license plates. You could barely walk without stepping on something or other. There were cars piled up four and five high on top of one another.

It was worse than Doris's room.

She took the left side and he went down the right. He was so busy watching where he walked that he forgot all about looking for the cricket ball.

The further away from the fence he got, the more junk there was. And the more junk there was, the less he got to see of Doris.

"Here it is! I've found it!"

He could hear her, but where was she? There was an old truck beside him. It sounded as if—

"I've got it!" Doris called out again.

She must have been just on the other side. Well, it was too high to climb over, and too dirty to crawl under. He'd open the door and go through the cabin part.

He pulled himself up by the steering wheel.

Yuk! Ugh! He'd barged straight into a spider's web. Ugh! Ugh! Spiders everywhere. Campbell hated spiders.

He jumped across to the other door and—CRASH!

One of his legs disappeared.

It had gone straight through the floor. He was doing the splits for the first time in his life.

"Help, Doris! Help!"

"It wasn't the ball after all," Doris said, and opened the door.

"Doris! Help!"

"Where's your other leg?"

"Through the floor. I've lost it. I knew this was going to happen. I knew it, I knew it."

    Doris tried pulling him out, but the metal was so rusty it was all jagged, and Campbell yelled a lot whenever she tried.

    "I'm finished now," Campbell muttered.

    Doris tried turning him around, sort of like she was unscrewing the lid off a jar. But it was too tight around his leg.

    "It's the end," Campbell was saying. "I'll never get out of here now."

Doris crawled underneath the truck and tried pushing his leg up. It still didn't want to budge.

She even took off his shoe and sock and tried tickling him.

"Yeeoooooow! Don't tickle!"

"It's no good, I'll have to go get something from home."

"Don't leave me."

"I'll be back before you can whistle 'In the Mood.'"

Campbell didn't know "In the Mood." There wasn't anything else for him to do but wait.

He thought about his stamps for a while. But you can get sick of thinking about stamps. He tried talking to himself, but he couldn't think of anything to say.

He whistled for a long time, though. The trouble was, he only knew two songs all the way through—"Happy Birthday" and "Jingle Bells." He whistled them so many times that his lips began to hurt.

After a while, all he could do was hum. He was better at humming anyway.

It was beginning to get dark. The sun had dropped down behind the iron works wall about five hundred "Happy Birthday"'s ago. He didn't feel like whistling or humming anymore. All the car bits and pieces were changing as the light faded. Things were losing their shapes, and mixing in with everything else. It was getting hard to tell one thing from another.

Where was Doris? He was sure "In the Mood" didn't go on for this long. No song went on for hours.

The breeze dropped away. A streetlight blinked on up the block somewhere. It was quieter too. He could hear the cars creaking amongst themselves.

Then it was dark.

Campbell started thinking about spiders. They were probably all watching him. He tried not to think about them, but the harder he tried, the more he thought about them.

Spiders loved hanging about in old cars and trucks and things. He'd read that in his encyclopedia. There could be as many as ten or twenty thousand of them in there with him.

What a terrible thought!

All those hundreds and thousands of little hairy legs and big fat furry bodies. What if they weren't the type that just watched? What if they were the type that liked to walk over and have a closer look? He had to change the subject, stop thinking about them.

He began thinking about scorpions instead. There'd probably be a few of them around too. And if there was one thing worse than a spider, it was a—

There was a noise.

First a clanging, then a rattling. It sounded like a gate. The gate to the yard? Maybe it was Doris. She must have come back with the police.

The gate banged closed again. There was more rattling. Then a lot of rattling. Something clicked shut.

It was quiet again.

Doris must have been having trouble remembering where he was. Nothing looked the same in this darkness. Nothing looked like anything much, come to think of it.

"I'm over here!" Campbell called out.

There was no answer.

"Over here Doris!"

It worked that time. He could hear them knocking and spilling things over to get to him.

They were getting closer. Almost there. They'd found him. Doris jumped up behind him into the cabin, and Campbell turned around.

Oh! Doris had changed! This wasn't Doris! (Unless Doris was wearing a dog suit.)

It was Mr. Caruso's watch dog.

The biggest, wildest, nastiest, most bad-tempered, scariest, toughest, roughest, and ugliest dog Campbell had ever seen. That *anybody* had ever seen. And Campbell was practically sitting cheek to cheek with it.

He was mean.

He swallowed bones whole; he played fetch with solid iron bars; he sharpened his teeth chewing on old car bodies; he ate two cans of dog food every night and didn't need an opener; he walked over broken glass without flinching; he just had to glance at a cat and it would pack up and leave town; he slept on a bed of nuts and bolts; he wore a studded collar; he never smiled—and his name was Tiger.

He stood so high Campbell had to strain his neck to keep on looking up at him. He was skinny—his ribs stuck out like corrugated iron under his short coat. His face was marked with lots of little white scars—and what a mouth.

He half yawned and all Campbell could see were fangs and teeth and more fangs and teeth. It's a wonder he had any room for a tongue in there.

He hadn't moved. He just went on standing there, staring.

Campbell felt like he'd caught the flu. He tried swallowing, but there was something big inside his throat. He was hot. His stomach felt like he'd just swallowed a brick. He was uncomfortable. He wanted to shift positions, but he decided to put it off for a while. One wrong move and he was done for.

Campbell tried talking.

"Hello. I'm Campbell. I wouldn't be here if it wasn't for Doris. Do you know Doris?"

Tiger didn't answer.

"I mean, if it wasn't for my leg being stuck, I'd be at home."

He didn't even blink.

Well, he was certainly a good watch dog, Campbell thought. That's all he did: watch—and breathe all over you.

He had the worst breath Campbell had ever smelled. It came and went in hot strong gusts across his face. It was powerful enough to block up his nose for good. It was even worse than his dentist's, Dr. Braithwaite.

Campbell slipped. He was trying hard not to, but he couldn't stop himself. He was twisting around so much that the arm he'd been leaning on had dozed off and turned to rubber.

Tiger stiffened, and moved forward. He hadn't liked it. His top lip was pulled back so he could show off some of his teeth. Campbell couldn't do anything but look. His mouth had dropped open so wide he was almost hitting his chest with his chin. Some of those fangs were so long you could have pole vaulted on them.

Suddenly there was an earth tremor. A long, low, rumbling noise. It shook the truck.

It was Tiger growling.

If Campbell had been old enough to have any hair on his chest, it would have dropped right off there and then.

Where was Doris? That was what he wanted to know. Doris was home eating dinner, that was where Doris was. But it was probably for the best that Campbell didn't know that right then.

Campbell remembered something. He slipped a hand into one of his coat pockets, and there it was. He could feel it. His Emergency Rations. He'd been saving that cold sausage from the night before last's dinner in case of starvation.

Gradually... slowly... carefully... he broke off a piece and dropped it in front of Tiger.

Tiger didn't seem to think much of it. He looked at it, looked back at him. Maybe he didn't like sausages. Campbell thought everybody liked them.

Then without taking his eyes away from Campbell, Tiger stooped, scooped it up, and—whomp!—he'd thrown it down. Hadn't even bothered to chew it.

He gave Tiger some more. He was handing it across piece by piece. Campbell had had this thought, you see, that while Tiger was busy eating something else, he wouldn't be thinking about eating *him*.

But Tiger was getting excited. He was beginning to get pushy. If Campbell happened to be a bit slow breaking the next piece off, he'd start to quiver and twitch.

Campbell had another thought. Maybe it hadn't been such a good idea. What if Tiger thought they were Campbell's own fingers that he was breaking off and giving to him? It did look a little like a finger. What if he started thinking Campbell tasted like sausages?

Campbell had one piece left. And it wasn't all that big either. Tiger had moved up closer. Help! He was standing over him. He did like cold sausage after all. Campbell closed his eyes, hoped for the best, and tossed it in Tiger's direction.

It slid straight through between his legs, over the edge, and on to the ground. Tiger jumped out after it.

Still no sign of Doris anywhere.

He listened, but all he could hear was Tiger stomping and hunting around down there. Then that stopped too.

Silence. More silence.

Where was Tiger? The way he ate, he'd been down there long enough to get through a whole string of sausages.

He felt him. Oh no! His toes! Tiger was sniffing them. Oh no! He'd gone looking for more sausage and found his toes. All five of them were down there, dangling away. They probably looked more like sausages than his fingers did.

Doris had forgotten to put his shoe back on.

Campbell was almost fainting. If it wasn't for the spiders he might have squashed, he probably would have.

Tiger was going over his toes from one end to the other. Slobbering over them with his wet nose, panting on them with his hot breath.

He was selecting a toe.

The big one? No, no, too tough. The little toe? Tasty, but too small. How about something in between, then?

Campbell couldn't stand it a moment longer. His toes weren't sausages!

Without thinking, he leapt up. He hit his head on the steering wheel, and knocked his elbow against the door.

Hey! His leg had budged. It was free! He could pull it out! It meant tearing his pants, but he didn't even notice that. There were too many other noises.

Barking, yelling, whooping, spiders running to get out of the way, Campbell bumping and rolling all over the place, more barking, spider collisions, thumping.

So much of it, that a little tear went unnoticed.

Campbell jumped out of the truck and ran.

Past old engines sprawled here, there and everywhere, he hurdled over bits of car bodies, dodged a broken crankshaft, tripped over a drum of oil, stubbed his toes about a thousand times, took three wrong turns, ran straight into a 1968 Buick, stepped in something very squishy, hit his head on something or other sticking out, tore his shirt and lost all his buttons except the top one, and lost almost his entire baseball card collection (out of his back pocket) before he found the fence.

It didn't look the same. He'd come out on the other side of the yard somewhere.

"Here I am! Over here!"

It was Doris! He'd almost forgotten about Doris. She was standing on the outside. She'd changed her clothes and everything.

"Tiger," Campbell puffed, "Mr. Caruso's dog is after me."

"I've brought you a ladder to escape on. It's up here."

Campbell ran along the fence following Doris. It was right across the other side of the block. Tiger must have seen him by now. Still, it was a ladder.

"Here it is!" Doris yelled out.

It was leaning up on the wrong side of the fence. Just perfect if you were trying to escape in instead of out.

Campbell had no choice. Tiger was gaining. He could hear him woofing and pounding along behind him. Campbell started up the fence—and he would have made it too, if Tiger hadn't known how to jump, and if the ladder had been on the right side, and if he hadn't kept on getting his foot stuck in the fence, and if he hadn't been wearing his coat. But Tiger had, and the ladder wasn't, and his foot did, and he was wearing his coat.

Tiger grabbed a mouthful of it. He wouldn't let go. If it hadn't been such a good coat it probably would have torn. And if it hadn't been such a good coat Campbell wouldn't have minded so much. But this was his favorite coat. He'd waited through two birthdays and a Christmas to get that coat.

"Take off the coat!" Doris was saying. Easy for her to say.

"No. I like it!"

"It's the only way."
"He can't have it."
"All he wants is your coat, Cam—
"He's not going to get it."

But he did. Campbell's arms go
were so tired he only just made it t

fainted

He stepped on to the ladder. Whoaaaaaaaaa!
It creaked, cracked, spli-i-i-t, creaked some more, and broke. The wood was so rotten that the rungs all smashed into little pieces.
All he was left holding on to were the two long side parts. For almost a whole minute he managed to keep his balance, swaying this way and that.
Trying not to step on Doris, watching out for the fence, looking out for gutters, missing poles…

He hit the parked car though. He landed on its roof.

Doris was clapping.

"Fantastic," she said, "you were better than the stilt man at the Moomba parade."

Campbell didn't care. He'd never seen the stilt man at the Moomba parade and he never wanted to. All he wanted was to go back home and try to move the Great Barrier Reef off the Grampian Mountains.

"You didn't happen to see my ball in there, did you?" Doris asked.

Campbell was too tired to answer.

"Oh well, don't worry about it. I've still got another one."

She would have to say that.

There was only more trouble for Campbell at home. His father was out, but his mother wasn't. She didn't believe him.

Not even the torn shirt, or the missing shoe, or that his coat was gone, or his one-legged pair of pants, or the bumps on his head, or his swollen knee were enough to convince her.

"I've been out fighting a wild dog," he said.

"Don't tell fibs," she said. "You've been out playing marbles with Robert again, haven't you?"

Marbles!

He didn't even *have* any marbles.

He had to spend the next three weekends in his room. *That* was good news at least.

"Unless Doris comes over," his mother added. "You can only go out if it's with Doris."

No it wasn't.